In the Beginning God
Created the Earth...

the Rivers

The Bible Tells Me So Press

In the Beginning God Created the Earth...
the Rivers

A children's book produced by
The Bible Tells Me So Press

Copyright © 2021
The Bible Tells Me So Corporation

All rights reserved. No part of this book, neither text nor illustrations, may be reproduced without permission in writing by the publisher.

PUBLISHED BY
THE BIBLE TELLS ME SO CORPORATION
WWW.THEBIBLETELLSMESO.COM

Second Printing, February 2025

The water that God created often flows in long and beautiful...

rivers!

Rivers can be calm and relaxing.

They also can be strong and powerful.

Sometimes a river flows over a cliff. When that happens, it makes...

a waterfall.

Rivers are formed in a lot of ways.

They can be formed by water
that comes up from the earth,
like from a spring.

They can also be formed when rain or snow falls high up in the mountains.

When
   that water
      begins to flow
         downhill, it starts
   to gather together
   as little streams.

When those streams merge together they become bigger and bigger until they form a river.

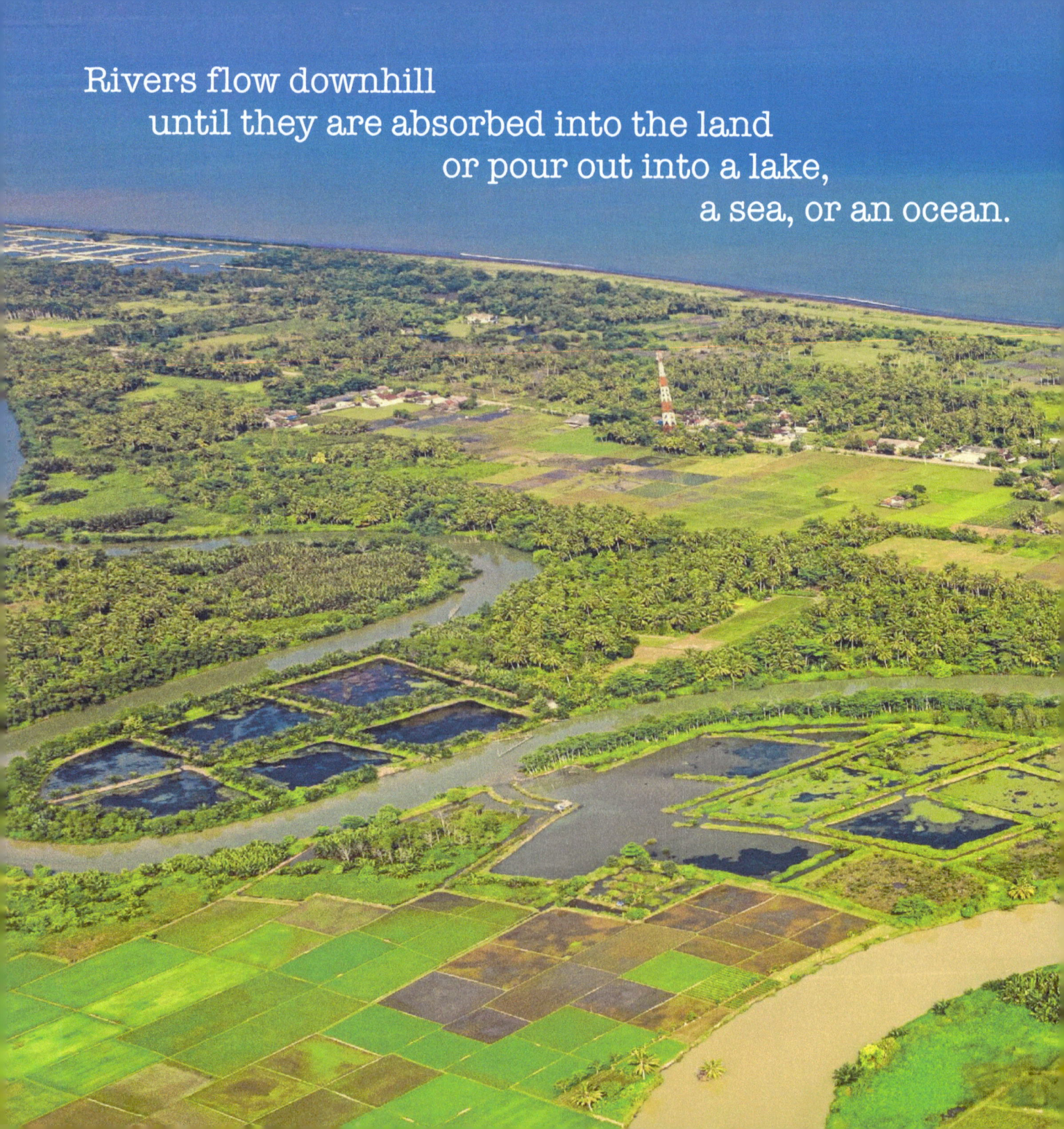
Rivers flow downhill until they are absorbed into the land or pour out into a lake, a sea, or an ocean.

The mighty Amazon River in South America flows over 55 million gallons of water into the Atlantic Ocean every second.

That's enough water to fill over 700 Olympic-size swimming pools in just the time it took you to read this sentence!

That's a lot of water!

Rivers can travel a long way.

The Nile River runs for over 4,100 miles!

It starts at Lake Victoria in Uganda and goes all the way to the Mediterranean Sea in Egypt.

That's almost long enough to flow completely across the United States and halfway back!

UNITED

The length of the Nile River

MEXICO

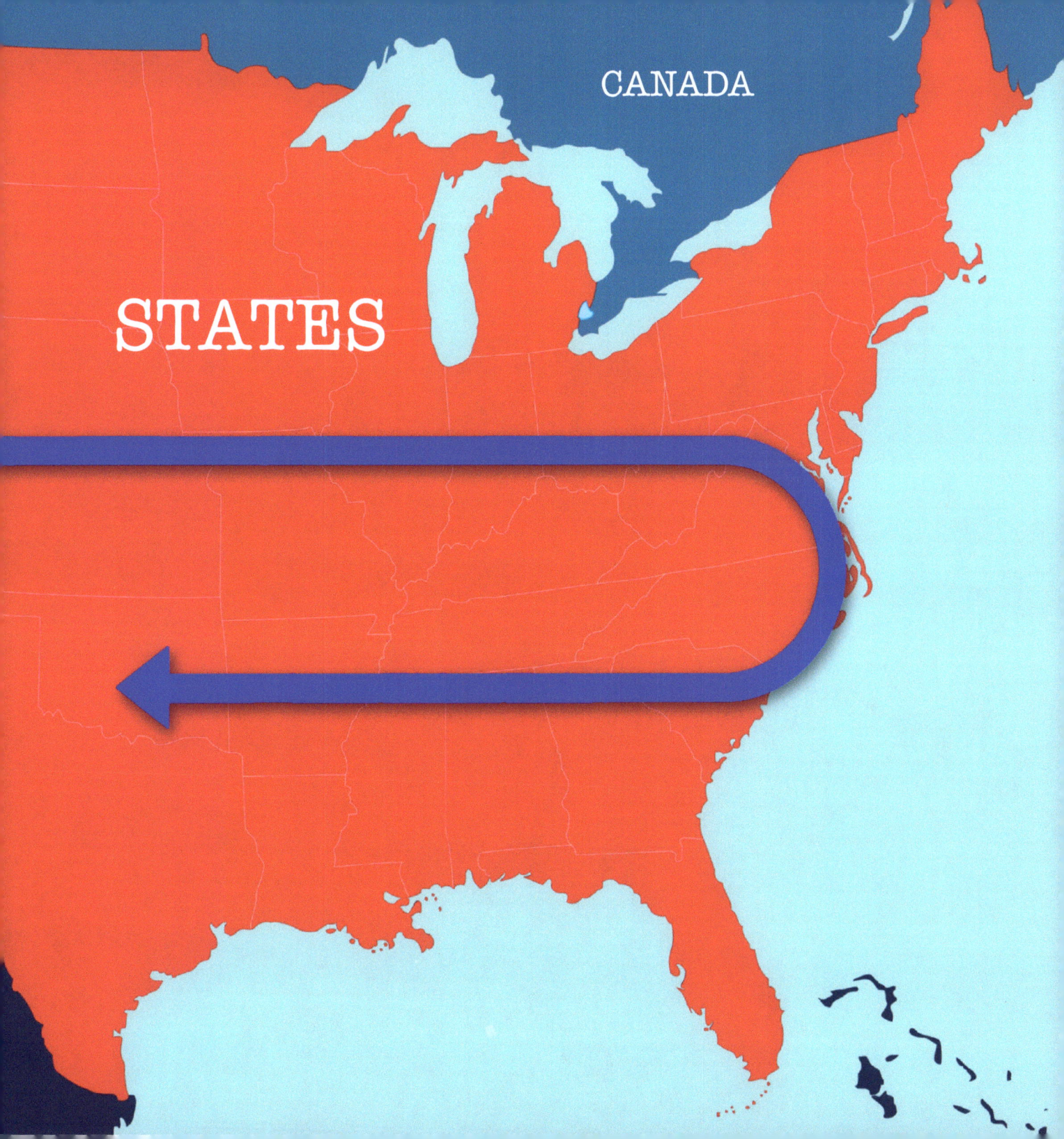

Animals depend on rivers to live. Many kinds of fish live in rivers.

And other animals depend on rivers for food and shelter.

These bears came to the river to search for food.

These beavers make their homes, called lodges, by weaving sticks, grass, and mud together in or around rivers.

Did you know that we need rivers too?

Many of us use water that flows down rivers to reach us.

Rivers also help us grow the food that we eat.

We dig canals in the ground
to bring water from rivers
to the farms and orchards
where we grow our food.

Rivers also make it easy to move things from one place

to another.

for a very long time.

So, the next time
you take a drink of water
or eat something grown
on a farm,

take a moment
to stop and thank the Lord
for giving us...

All the rivers run to the sea,
yet the sea is not full;
to the place where the rivers run,
there they run again.

Ecclesiastes 1:7

For more
books, videos, songs, and crafts,
visit us online at
TheBibleTellsMeSo.com

Standing on the Bible and growing!

www.ingramcontent.com/pod-product-compliance
Lightning Source LLC
Chambersburg PA
CBHW041534040426
42446CB00002B/86